**OSTRICH PUBLISHERS**

Published by Ostrich Publishing Group

Charlotte, North Carolina 28212, U.S.A

First published in the United States of America by Ostrich Publishing Group, an Independent Book publisher.

9798395556516

Copyright © 2022 Ostrich Publishers

www.ostrichpress.com

All rights reserved.

ISBN: 9798395556516

Except in the United States of America, this book is sold subject to the conditions that is shall not, by way of trade or otherwise, be lent, re-sold, hired out, or otherwise circulated without the publisher's prior consent in any form of binding or cover other than in which is it published and without a similar condition including this condition being imposed on the subsequent purchaser.

# THE MAGIC OF DIRECT MAIL

***Dedicated** To every entrepreneur who dares to dream and works tirelessly to turn those dreams into reality.*

*To those who embrace innovation while cherishing the magic of traditional methods.*

*And to the incredible team at Salesfully.com, whose unwavering commitment and support have been instrumental in penning this book. This work is dedicated to you all.*

*May you continue to inspire, disrupt, and make a difference.*

# TABLE OF CONTENTS

*A Note to you, the reader* — 12

*Preface* — 16

*Chapter 1: Understanding the Direct Mail Landscape.* — 19

*Chapter 2: In Pursuit of the Mail-Happy Prospect* — 24

*Chapter 3: Finding the Holy Grail: Products and Services for Direct Mail Success* — 31

*Chapter 4: Crafting Your Direct Mail Strategy* — 39

*Chapter 5: Powell's Books: A Direct Mail Triumph* — 53

*Chapter 6: Your Step-by-Step Guide to Direct Mail Success* — 59

*Chapter 7: Measuring and Optimizing Your Direct Mail Campaign* — 66

*Chapter 8: The Future* — 72

*Conclusion: Your Journey to Direct Mail Success* — 79

*Appendix: Resources and Further Reading* — 84

*About the Author - Frank Dappah* — 94

## A Note to You, My Fellow Entrepreneur, the Fearless Voyager

Hello there, adventurous soul! Welcome aboard the exhilarating, heart-thumping, sometimes dizzying, but always rewarding ride of entrepreneurship. And who am I to be your tour guide, you might ask?

Well, let's see, in this vibrant circus of entrepreneurship, I've taken on a myriad of roles - the daring acrobat, the steady tightrope walker, and occasionally, yes, the light-hearted clown (and boy, do we need humor in this business!).

My name is Frank Dappah, a small business owner, an entrepreneur, an author, and above all, a lifelong learner who's absolutely smitten with his work: Building my business, investing in others, and sharing all I've learned on this incredible journey.

Here's a little background on me: I hail from the beautiful country of Ghana but made the United States my home as a youngster.

I grew up on the streets of Philadelphia and eventually took roots in Charlotte, NC, where I started my Insurance sales agency. Success, as they say, begets success. So, it wasn't long before my wife, Bernice, and I launched Salesfully.com, a game-changing sales discovery platform tailor-made for budget-conscious startups and small businesses.

Along the way, I've penned over 200 books - yes, you read it right, over 200! From sales to business, personal growth to children's books, you could say I've got a library of my own. Every now and then, I take a breather from my usual subjects to share my observations about the fascinating world around me.

Now, before we go any further, I must lay down a disclaimer: I'm not a mental health sage, a philosopher, a social scientist, or a legal expert. Heck, I wouldn't even classify myself as a Thinker with a capital 'T'.

I am simply a student of life, observing the world around me and sharing what I've learned with all of you. While I relish sharing my experiences, do keep in mind that they are not intended to be professional advice. If you need specialized help, it's always best to consult with certified professionals.

So, dear reader, neither I nor my publisher can be held responsible for what unfolds in your personal or business life as a result of you diving headfirst into my pool of thoughts. They are just that - thoughts. Musings of a well-meaning entrepreneur hoping to sprinkle some wisdom and cheer along the way.

Good luck, and here's to a journey of discovery!

**Frank Dappah**

# PREFACE

As you embark on this expedition through "The Magic of Direct Mail: Revitalizing Business with Direct Mail Magic," I welcome you with open arms and a brimming quill. This book, my friends, is much more than a collection of words.

It's a handcrafted mosaic of tales, lessons, insights, and above all, an enduring love for the often overlooked, yet surprisingly potent tool of business - Direct Mail.

Yes, you read it right. Direct Mail. In an age where our lives are ensconced in the digital world, where email and social media dictate our communication, the charm of a physical piece of mail holds its ground. It's a testament to the power of human touch, an embodiment of personal communication, and a silent warrior in the world of marketing.

This book is my journey into exploring the forgotten art and science of Direct Mail. It's a journey that takes us back in time, and then, interestingly, right back into the future. It's an exploration of how a tool from the past remains relevant, potent, and magical in an era obsessed with speed and technology.

You might be wondering, why Direct Mail? Isn't it outdated, slow, and ineffective? My friends, this book is my response to these questions. As we navigate through its chapters, we will uncover the unique advantages of Direct Mail, its potential to reach and engage audiences in a way digital mediums can't, and how, when used with creativity and strategy, it can be a powerful engine for business growth.

Prepare yourself to dive into real-world case studies, practical strategies, step-by-step guides, and personal anecdotes. Together, we will unlock the secrets of Direct Mail, learning how to harness its power to not just survive, but thrive in the competitive business landscape.

But before we delve into these pages, a word of caution - be ready to challenge your assumptions, rethink your strategies, and most importantly, embrace the unconventional.

After all, isn't that what entrepreneurship is all about? So, buckle up and get ready for an exciting journey into the world of Direct Mail. Trust me, it's going to be magical.

## CHAPTER ONE
# Understanding the Direct Mail Landscape.

Ah, the history of Direct Mail - it's a story that's as old as civilization itself. From ancient Egyptians carving promotional messages on wooden slabs to the mass production of catalogs in the 1800s to personalized mailers in the 21st century, Direct Mail has evolved alongside humanity, proving its resilience time and time again.

Our journey into the annals of Direct Mail takes us back over 4000 years. Yes, you read that right - the origins of Direct Mail trace back to the flourishing civilizations of Ancient Egypt. Merchants carved their offers onto wooden slabs and distributed them across the population, making it one of the earliest recorded instances of Direct Mail marketing.

Fast forward to the industrial revolution, and you'll find the seeds of modern Direct Mail taking root. With the advent of printing technology, businesses began mass-producing catalogs and leaflets, distributing them far and wide. Names like Sears and Montgomery Ward became household entities, thanks to their extensive Direct Mail campaigns.

Come the 20th century, Direct Mail evolved further. From generic leaflets, it transformed into personalized mailers, employing user data to create customized messages that resonated with the recipients. Companies leveraged emerging technologies to reach their customers in more engaging, relatable ways.

## Why Direct Mail in the Digital Era?

If the history of Direct Mail is a testament to its enduring appeal, its relevance in the digital era is a proof of its adaptability. Despite the deluge of digital marketing channels, Direct Mail has not only managed to hold its ground but has also found unique ways to outperform digital mediums.

Why? It all boils down to one key factor: sensory engagement. Unlike digital marketing, which mainly engages the visual sense, Direct Mail appeals to multiple senses - sight, touch, and sometimes even smell and sound. This multi-sensory engagement triggers emotional responses, making the communication more memorable and persuasive.

Moreover, Direct Mail stands out in a cluttered digital landscape. With inboxes overflowing with promotional emails and social media feeds bombarded with ads, a piece of physical mail comes as a refreshing change. It captures attention, commands engagement, and leaves a lasting impression.

In a time when customers crave personalized experiences, Direct Mail delivers in spades. It allows businesses to create hyper-personalized messages, tailored to each recipient's preferences and behaviors. In fact, according to a study by InfoTrends, 84% of consumers are more likely to open a piece of mail if it's personalized.

Add to this the fact that Direct Mail boasts a higher response rate compared to email, and you've got a formidable marketing tool that's perfect for the digital era. According to the Direct Marketing Association, Direct Mail's response rate is 4.4%, compared to email's measly 0.12%.

In a nutshell, Direct Mail in the digital era is not just relevant; it's indispensable. It offers the personal touch of the old world, combined with the data-driven capabilities of the new. It's a magic potion that can bring your brand to life, engage your customers on a deeper level, and drive your business forward.

## CHAPTER TWO

# In Pursuit of the Mail-Happy Prospect

**"Friends" or "Game of Thrones" - Knowing Your Prospects.**

Understanding the essence of your ideal prospect is like picking between watching "Friends" or "Game of Thrones" - two wildly different yet intriguing options, each appealing in their own ways.

Your Direct Mail campaign is no different. So, are your prospects Central Perk coffee-lovers or die-hard dragon fanatics?

**Digital Junkies vs. Paper Huggers**

It's time to separate the wheat from the chaff, or should I say, digital addicts from paper enthusiasts. Are your prospects living in the matrix of the digital world, or do they cherish the feel of paper between their fingers? Direct Mail certainly has a soft spot for the latter!

## Enter Charlie: A Direct Mail Success Story.

Consider the tale of Charlie, the rural Montana craftsman. Facing the challenges of limited internet access, Charlie leveraged the power of Direct Mail to transform his handmade furniture business, proving that sometimes, the old school ways can be game changers.

## Age: Is it Just a Number in Direct Mail?

If you're targeting a prospect who still gets excited about the mailman's arrival and the sound of envelopes dropping into the mailbox, chances are they aren't millennials. Spoiler Alert: Baby Boomers and Silent Generation folks are your best bet here!

## A Surprise Twist in the Direct Mail Tale!

Just when you thought you had your prospects figured out, here comes the plot twist - the younger generation, the supposed torchbearers of all things digital, are showing an increasing preference for less digital means of consuming data. What a surprise, eh?

This isn't just a statement plucked out of thin air; we've got the stats to back it up!

**The Statistical Rabbit Hole**

1. According to a study by Mailmen UK, 84% of millennials take the time to look through their physical mail, providing a golden opportunity for businesses to catch their attention via Direct Mail.

2. Data from a Gallup poll shows that 36% of people under the age of 30 look forward to checking their mailboxes each day. In fact, the younger the individual, the more likely they are to read Direct Mail rather than discard it.

3. A study conducted by the United States Postal Service found that millennials, who are often bombarded with digital advertisements, consider physical mail a

novelty and enjoy receiving it.

4. Market research firm InfoTrends discovered that 63% of Gen Z, who are known for their short attention spans, were more likely to remember information they received by mail rather than email.

5. A report by the Data & Marketing Association (DMA) found that Direct Mail's response rates are actually 10 to 30 times higher than that of digital.

## Less Digital, More Direct: A New Opportunity.

These stats paint a clear picture. Younger generations, tired of the digital clutter, are increasingly leaning towards less digital means of consuming data.

And this, my friends, is an excellent opportunity for Direct Mail. It's like finding an oasis in the digital desert.

With the right message and a creative approach, Direct Mail can effectively cut through the noise to reach younger prospective customers. It's the classic tortoise and the hare scenario. While digital advertising is sprinting away, Direct Mail, slow and steady, is capturing the attention of the younger audience, proving that sometimes the traditional ways can lead to the finish line.

So, next time you're planning a Direct Mail campaign, don't forget these young enthusiasts. They might just be your star customers in the making!

**Building Relationships, One Letter at a Time.**

And finally, if you are hoping to create connections that are as warm and fuzzy as a teddy bear on Valentine's Day, Direct Mail is your go-to. The perfect prospect here is the one who cherishes such heartwarming, personal interactions.

Now, that's what we call a Direct Mail persona sketch - fun, informative, and painted with a broad brush of humor. So, put on your thinking cap, or maybe your Sorting Hat, and identify which house your prospect belongs to!

And once we've identified our prospects, let's dive into the next chapter - "Products and Services: The Direct Mail Darlings."

## CHAPTER THREE

# Finding the Holy Grail: Products and Services for Direct Mail Success

**Navigating the Maze Runner of Products**

Finding the right products for a Direct Mail campaign can feel like being Thomas in "The Maze Runner" - there are seemingly endless possibilities, and each turn you take leads to another labyrinth. But fret not! We're here to provide you with the compass to navigate this maze.

1. **The Classics Never Go Out of Style:** Printed catalogs, brochures, and leaflets have been the Harry Potters of Direct Mail - timeless and ever-loved. They offer comprehensive details about a product or service and give customers a tangible feel for your brand. Think IKEA catalogs - a true icon in the Direct Mail world.
2. **The Big Reveal - Unboxing:** This one's for businesses selling physical products.

Send a miniature or a sample of your product. It's like the exciting feeling of unboxing a new phone or unwrapping a present, and who doesn't love that? This approach worked brilliantly for Birchbox, a beauty subscription box service. They literally put their product in the hands (and mailboxes) of prospects!

3. **The Powerful Persuaders - Coupons:** Ah, the humble coupon. These little pieces of paper are persuasive! They create urgency and offer a tangible incentive to purchase. It's the closest you can get to saying, "Come to the dark side; we have discounts!"

## The Services Star Wars

Not a product-based business? No problem! The force is strong with Direct Mail in the service industry as well.

1. **The Subtle Reminder - Postcards:** Postcards are like that friend who nudges you gently when you're about to forget something. A postcard reminder about an upcoming dental cleaning or

oil change might be the only thing standing between you and a toothache or a car breakdown.
2. **The Exclusives - VIP Invitations:** Remember how Charlie felt when he found the golden ticket in his Wonka bar? That's how your customers will feel when they receive an exclusive invite to your event or service. It makes them feel special, like they're part of the Avengers team.
3. **Story Time - Newsletters:** Who doesn't love a good story? Newsletters allow you to connect with your audience, tell them what's new and exciting, and keep your brand at the top of their minds. It's like a weekly episode of their favorite show!

## The "Chewy" Tale

Consider Chewy.com, an online pet retailer that has taken Direct Mail to another level. In addition to their regular marketing materials, they occasionally send their customers hand-painted portraits of their pets.

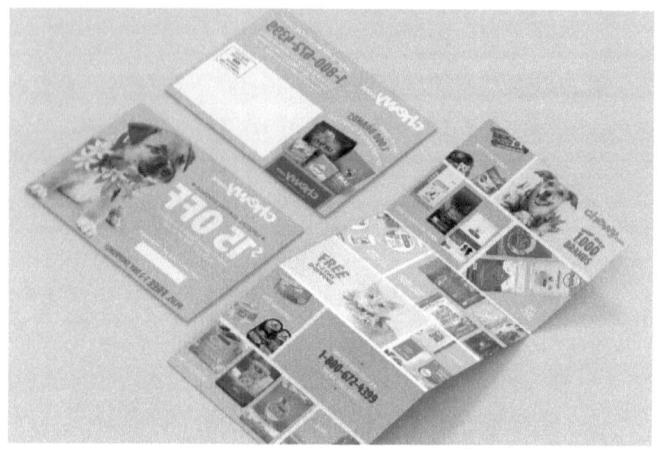

This personalized touch has not only delighted their customers but has also led to a torrent of free, positive social media attention. Talk about a purr-fect strategy!

**Harnessing Direct Mail Magic: Positioning Your Unique Startup Offerings!**

If you're a startup founder thinking, "Direct Mail sounds like Hogwarts, but my product/service isn't a tangible object, it's not an invitation to an event, or a coupon," stay with me. This section is your personal guide to turning your Patronus into a tangible reality (I promise, last Harry Potter reference…maybe). Let's dive into the ways you can creatively position your unique offerings for Direct Mail.

**The Software Sorcerer**

If you offer software or a digital service, don't despair! Your product may not be tangible, but its benefits are. Create a visually engaging postcard or brochure that presents the problem your software solves in an eye-catching, engaging manner.

Highlight testimonials, ratings, or even a cool infographic representing the benefits or features. Maybe even include a QR code linking to a demo or a special trial offer. Think of it as creating a tangible representation of your digital magic.

**Subscription Service Spellcasting**

If you run a subscription service, say, an online

yoga class platform or a premium newsletter, you're a wizard of recurring customer engagement. Use Direct Mail to extend that wizardry. Create a glossy flyer with captivating images showcasing what a subscriber gains—be it inner peace from doing a sun salutation or premium insights that help them achieve Wall Street stardom.

**The E-commerce Enchanter**

Are you the sorcerer of an e-commerce startup? Your Direct Mail can include product samples if they're small or low-cost. For larger items, high-quality product photos on a postcard can do the trick. Consider including a unique promo code to track response rates and encourage immediate action.

**Service-based Sorcery**

For service-based startups, whether you're a digital marketing wizard or a spellbinding graphic designer, you can use Direct Mail to present case studies, customer testimonials, or before-and-after scenarios. Translate your digital portfolio into a physical format that prospective customers can peruse at their leisure.

**Real-Life Magical Success: Headspace**

Take Headspace, the popular mindfulness and meditation app. On the surface, they might seem an unlikely candidate for Direct Mail success, but they've managed to translate their intangible service into a tangible marketing tool.

How? Through postcards highlighting the benefits of meditation, user testimonials, and a call-to-action offering a free trial to new users. It's a winning example of creatively adapting an unconventional offering for Direct Mail.

Remember, startups, in the Direct Mail world, you're only limited by your imagination. So, get creative, think outside the traditional Direct Mail box, and start casting your Direct Mail spells!

## CHAPTER FOUR
## Crafting Your Direct Mail Strategy

Ah, crafting your direct mail strategy—it's like putting together a puzzle, but instead of puzzle pieces, you have all these different elements to consider.

Let's dive into the nitty-gritty and unravel the mysteries of reaching your audience, building a compelling message, and making your design and presentation shine.

### Knowing Your Audience:

First things first, my fellow entrepreneur: you gotta know your audience like the back of your hand. Who are they? What do they want? What makes them tick?

Get inside their heads (not literally, of course—leave that to the neuroscientists) and figure out what drives them. Are they young and hip, or seasoned and sophisticated?

Are they obsessed with the latest trends, or do they prefer timeless classics? Understanding your audience will help you tailor your message and design your entire direct mail campaign to resonate with them on a deep level.

Knowing your audience is like having a secret superpower as an entrepreneur. It's the key that unlocks the door to their hearts, minds, and, most importantly, their wallets. You see, my friend, when you truly understand your audience, it's like having a direct line to their deepest desires and aspirations.

**So, how do you go about getting to know your audience?** Well, it starts with research—digging deep into their demographics, **interests**, and **behavior**. Are they young professionals seeking adventure and excitement, or perhaps busy parents looking for convenience and practicality? By unraveling these insights, you can create a detailed persona of your ideal customer, complete with a name, hobbies, and even a favorite movie (mine happens to be Back to the Future, by the way).

But it doesn't stop there, my fellow entrepreneur. Knowing your audience goes beyond just statistics and data. It's about getting into their mindset and understanding their pain points, aspirations, and what makes them tick. Imagine yourself as a detective, piecing together clues from social media, online forums, and customer feedback to uncover their deepest desires and challenges.

And here's the magical part: once you truly know your audience, you can speak their language. You can empathize with their struggles, connect with their dreams, and position your product or service as the answer they've been waiting for. It's like having a secret code that unlocks their trust and builds a genuine connection. There are tools out there like Esri (esri.com) that can help you dig deeper into the demographics in any particular geo-location as you embark on your direct mail journey.

But remember, my friend, audiences are not static beings. They evolve and change over time. So, it's crucial to keep your finger on the pulse of your audience's ever-shifting desires and preferences.

Stay tuned to the latest trends, engage in conversations, and be open to feedback. The more you stay connected, the better you can adapt your messaging, offerings, and even your overall brand to meet their evolving needs.

In the world of direct mail, knowing your audience is the secret ingredient to a successful campaign. It's like having a cosmic GPS that guides you to the hearts and mailboxes of the people who are most likely to be enchanted by what you have to offer. So, my dear entrepreneur, embrace the power of knowing your audience, and watch as your direct mail campaigns become irresistible invitations that your audience simply can't refuse.

**Building Your Message:**

Now that you know who you're talking to, it's time to build your message. Think of it as crafting a captivating story. You want to grab your reader's attention, engage their emotions, and leave them eagerly wanting more.

Be clear, concise, and compelling. Highlight the unique benefits of your product or service and show how it can solve their problems or fulfill their desires.

Remember, your message should be like a captivating movie trailer—tease, intrigue, and leave them craving the full experience.

Building your message is where the magic truly happens, my entrepreneurial friend. It's like being the master storyteller of your own blockbuster movie. Picture this: your audience is sitting on the edge of their seats, waiting for you to sweep them away on an unforgettable journey.

First things first, cut through the noise and clutter with a message that is laser-focused and easily digestible. Think of it as a punchy one-liner that instantly grabs attention. You want your audience to go, "Whoa, tell me more!"

But don't stop there, my friend. A captivating message is also about stirring emotions. Tap into the desires, dreams, and pain points of your audience. Are they yearning for more time, freedom, or success? Or perhaps they're seeking joy, adventure, or a sense of belonging. Whatever it may be, connect with their emotions on a deep level.

Now, here's the secret sauce: highlight the unique benefits of your product or service.

What sets you apart from the competition? How will your offering make their lives better, easier, or more extraordinary?

Paint a vivid picture of the transformation they can experience by choosing you. Show, don't just tell, how your solution can solve their problems or fulfill their wildest dreams.

And remember, my fellow entrepreneur, storytelling is an art. Infuse your message with personality, authenticity, and a sprinkle of humor when appropriate. Be relatable, and let your passion shine through. People connect with stories, so make yours unforgettable.

As I have said many times before, think of your message as a movie trailer, my friend. Tease your audience, intrigue them, and leave them begging for the full experience. Leave them wanting more, eagerly anticipating the next chapter of your story.

And as you craft your message, keep in mind the power of repetition. Reinforce your key points, but in different ways and through various mediums. Repetition is the secret ingredient to making your message stick.

So, my dear entrepreneur, embrace the art of building your message. Let it be a symphony of words and emotions that resonates deeply with your audience. And as you weave your tale, always remember that you have the power to captivate, inspire, and leave a lasting impact on those who encounter your message. Lights, camera, action!

**Design and Presentation:**

Design and presentation, my friend, is where we unleash the power of visual allure. It's time to make your direct mail piece a sight to behold, a masterpiece that demands attention. Imagine it as an art gallery showcasing your brand's unique style and captivating your audience with its sheer beauty.

Now, don't be afraid to let your creativity soar. Colors, fonts, and imagery should all work in harmony to create a visual experience that speaks directly to your target audience.

Think about what appeals to them, what catches their eye, and what aligns with your brand's personality. It's like curating a collection that leaves a lasting impression.

Remember, my fellow entrepreneur, presentation is everything. Pay attention to every little detail, like the quality of the paper you choose, the way your mail piece is folded and packaged.

Each element should be meticulously crafted to create a sensory experience that your audience can't resist. It's like a carefully wrapped gift, enticing them to unveil the magic within.

**But here's the secret sauce:** stay true to your unique style. Just like a fashion show, you want to dress to impress while maintaining your authenticity. Let your brand's personality shine through the design and presentation. Be bold, be memorable, and be unmistakably you. After all, it's your brand's moment in the spotlight. And don't forget the power of storytelling through visuals. Every image, every graphic should serve a purpose and evoke emotion.

Use visuals to reinforce your message, to create intrigue, and to leave a lasting impression. A picture is worth a thousand words, my friend, so choose them wisely.

As you craft your design and presentation, think about the overall experience you want to create. How will your audience feel when they receive your direct mail piece?

Will they be delighted, intrigued, or inspired? Aim to create a sensory journey that captures their attention from the moment they lay eyes on your mail piece until the very last detail.

So, my fellow startup-er, let your creativity run wild and transform your direct mail into a visual masterpiece. Pay attention to every element of design and presentation, from colors and fonts to the way it's packaged. Let it be a reflection of your brand's personality, and an irresistible invitation for your audience to engage with your message.

Get ready to dazzle and captivate with design that leaves a lasting impression. Onward, to visual glory!

**In my experience**, an astounding 88% of people pause to examine mail that catches their eye when they sift through their mail at the end of the day.

It's that golden opportunity to make a lasting impression and introduce your new products or services to your desired audience. So, my friend, let's create direct mail pieces that truly pop in terms of visuals and grab attention like a shooting star in the night sky.

When designing your direct mail, remember that eye-catching visuals are key. Use vibrant colors, captivating images, and bold typography to make your mailer stand out from the sea of envelopes. And here's a pro tip: prominently display any promotional offers in big, bold font where they're easily visible. Let your audience know that there's something exciting waiting for them inside.

**But that's not all.** Don't be afraid to leverage the power of the United States Postal Service's " Every Door Direct Mail" service. With this service, you can strategically target specific neighborhoods and have your mail delivered right to the doorsteps of your desired prospective customers. It's like having a personal invitation to their homes, enticing them to explore what you have to offer.

Seize the opportunity to make a visual impact with your direct mail. Catch the attention of your audience when they least expect it, and leave a memorable impression that lingers long after they've checked their mail. It's your time to shine and stand out from the crowd. Let's create direct mail that leaves no mailbox untouched and no customer unengaged.

## CHAPTER FIVE
## Powell's Books: A Direct Mail Triumph

Powell's Books, an iconic independent bookstore based in Portland, Oregon, serves as an inspiring case study in the realm of direct mail success. Facing challenges such as declining foot traffic and intense competition from online retailers, Powell's Books embarked on a strategic direct mail campaign that not only reinvigorated their customer base but also solidified their position as a beloved local institution.

Powell's Books understood the importance of capturing the attention and imagination of their target audience. They recognized that direct mail offered a unique opportunity to engage readers in a tactile and personal way, creating a sense of excitement and anticipation that digital platforms often struggle to replicate.

Let's explore how Powell's Books achieved their direct mail triumph through a combination of thoughtful strategy, compelling content, and targeted distribution.

**Crafting Compelling Content**

At the heart of Powell's Books' direct mail success lies their ability to craft compelling content that resonates with their audience. They understand that book lovers crave more than just a transaction—they seek a connection, an experience that transports them to new worlds and sparks their intellectual curiosity. Powell's Books tailored their direct mail pieces to reflect this understanding.

Their mailers featured captivating book recommendations tailored to each recipient's reading history and preferences. By leveraging their extensive knowledge of their customers' past purchases, Powell's Books curated personalized book suggestions that enticed readers to explore new titles and authors.

This personalized approach not only showcased their expertise but also demonstrated a genuine interest in meeting each customer's unique literary interests.

Powell's Books collaborated with local artists and illustrators to create visually stunning mailers that celebrated the beauty and charm of Portland.

These artistic collaborations not only added a touch of local flair but also showcased Powell's Books as a cultural hub deeply rooted in the community. The mailers became collectors' items in their own right, encouraging recipients to keep and display them, further extending the reach and impact of Powell's Books' direct mail campaign.

**Targeted Distribution and Measuring Success**

Powell's Books understood the importance of targeting their direct mail campaign to reach the most receptive audience.

They used data analysis and segmentation techniques to identify specific customer segments based on demographics, reading preferences, and past purchase history. By tailoring their mailers to these segments, Powell's Books ensured that their messages resonated with the right recipients, maximizing the likelihood of engagement and response.

To measure the success of their direct mail campaign, Powell's Books tracked key metrics such as response rate, conversion rate, and foot traffic. By utilizing unique offer codes or coupons specific to the direct mail campaign, they were able to track and attribute responses directly to their mailers. This data-driven approach provided valuable insights into the campaign's effectiveness, allowing Powell's Books to make informed decisions and refine their strategies for future initiatives.

Powell's Books' direct mail triumph exemplifies the power of thoughtful strategy, compelling content, and targeted distribution. By understanding their audience, crafting personalized content, and measuring success, Powell's Books revitalized their customer base, strengthened their brand, and redefined the bookstore experience in the digital age. Their success serves as an inspiration for businesses seeking to harness the potential of direct mail to engage customers, foster connections, and drive tangible results.

## CHAPTER SIX
# Your Step-by-Step Guide to Direct Mail Success

**Get Ready to Soar!**

Successful direct mail campaigns require careful strategizing and preparation. Start by clearly defining your goals and objectives. What do you want to achieve with your campaign? *Increased sales? Brand awareness? Customer retention?* Knowing your desired outcomes will guide your decision-making process and shape your campaign's direction.

*For example:*

Imagine you're launching a new product line targeting health-conscious consumers. Your goal is to increase product sales by 20% within three months. With this objective in mind, you can now delve into market research and customer segmentation. Analyze consumer behavior, preferences, and demographics to identify your target audience.

For instance, you might find that your ideal customers are primarily millennials who prioritize organic and sustainable products. Armed with this information, you can tailor your messaging and design to resonate specifically with this audience.

**Building Your Direct Mail: The Art of Captivating Creativity**

Now that you've done your planning

groundwork, it's time to let your creativity run wild and build your direct mail masterpiece. Your direct mail piece should be a visual feast that grabs attention, engages emotions, and leaves a lasting impression. But you already knew that, right?

Think about your target audience and what will resonate with them. Consider their interests, values, and pain points. Use eye-catching colors, fonts, and imagery that align with your brand and captivate your recipients. Don't forget to craft a compelling message that highlights the unique benefits of your product or service. Think of it as creating a story that your audience can't resist. Just like we discussed before.

*For example:*

Let's continue with our previous example. To appeal to health-conscious millennials, your direct mail design could feature vibrant, nature-inspired visuals, showcasing the freshness and sustainability of your products.

Use modern and clean fonts to convey a sense of trust and authenticity. Include compelling copy that emphasizes the health benefits, ethical sourcing, and social responsibility of your brand.

By aligning your design and message with your target audience's values and aspirations, you're more likely to capture their attention and generate a positive response.

## Executing Your Campaign: The Moment of Truth

It's showtime, my friends! The execution of your direct mail campaign is where all your hard work pays off. Pay attention to every detail, from printing to postage. Ensure that your mailers are of high quality, well-designed, and flawlessly executed.

Timing is also crucial. Consider the

seasonality and trends in your industry, and schedule your mailings accordingly.

Remember, consistency and frequency are key to staying top-of-mind with your audience. And don't forget to track and measure the results of your campaign. Monitor response rates, conversion rates, and customer feedback to gain valuable insights and make informed decisions for future campaigns.

*For Example:*

Let's say you've executed your direct mail campaign and received a 10% response rate, surpassing your initial goal. This is a fantastic result, but the journey doesn't end there. Dig deeper into the data to understand which elements of your campaign resonated most with your audience.

Analyze response rates among different customer segments, geographic locations, or promotional offers. This information will help you fine-tune your future campaigns and maximize your return on investment.

By meticulously planning your campaign, unleashing your creativity, and executing flawlessly, you're setting yourself up for direct mail success. Remember, direct mail offers a tangible and personalized experience that can make a powerful impact on your target audience. So, my friends, grab your planning toolkit, let your creative juices flow, and execute your direct mail campaign with confidence. Measure your results, learn from the data, and make adjustments as needed. Direct mail has the power to cut through the digital noise and create meaningful connections with your audience. So, don't hesitate to leverage this tried-and-true marketing channel to drive success for your business.

## CHAPTER SEVEN

# Measuring and Optimizing Your Direct Mail Campaign

Congratulations, my savvy entrepreneur, on successfully executing your direct mail campaign! But the journey doesn't end there. In Chapter 7, we dive into the crucial task of measuring and optimizing your campaign to maximize its impact and achieve even greater success.

### 1. Key Performance Indicators (KPIs)

Tracking the right Key Performance Indicators (KPIs) is essential to gauge the effectiveness of your direct mail campaign. These metrics provide valuable insights into the performance and return on investment (ROI) of your efforts. Some important KPIs to consider include:

- **Response Rate:** Measure the percentage of recipients who responded to your direct mail piece, such as by making a purchase, requesting more information, or taking a desired action. This indicates the level of engagement and interest generated by your campaign.
- **Conversion Rate:** Determine the percentage of responders who converted into customers or took a desired action, such as subscribing to a service or attending an event. This metric reflects the effectiveness of your direct mail in driving desired outcomes.
- **Cost per Acquisition:** Calculate the cost incurred to acquire a new customer

through your direct mail campaign. This metric helps assess the efficiency and cost-effectiveness of your marketing efforts.

## 2. Learning from Your Campaign

Analyzing the data and insights gathered from your direct mail campaign is crucial for learning and improvement. Here's how you can make the most of this valuable information:

- **A/B Testing:** Experiment with different variables in your direct mail pieces, such as headlines, offers, designs, or formats, and compare their performance. This allows you to identify what resonates best with your audience and optimize future campaigns.
- **Customer Feedback:** Solicit feedback from your recipients to gain insights into their perceptions, preferences, and suggestions. This direct input can provide valuable guidance for refining your messaging, offers, or targeting strategies.
- **Tracking Codes:** Use unique tracking codes or personalized URLs to attribute

responses or conversions to specific mail pieces or segments. This enables you to measure the effectiveness of individual components and make data-driven decisions for optimization.

### 3. Continuous Improvement

Optimizing your direct mail campaign is an ongoing process. It requires a commitment to continuous improvement and a willingness to adapt. Here are some key practices to keep in mind:

- **Test, Test, Test:** Continuously test and iterate on various elements of your campaign, including messaging, offers, visuals, and targeting strategies. Embrace a culture of experimentation and use the insights gained to refine your approach.
- **Integration with Other Channels:** Explore how direct mail can complement and integrate with your other marketing channels, such as email, social media, or online advertising. By creating a cohesive and multi-channel marketing strategy, you can amplify your message

and engage your audience more effectively.
- **Data Analysis and Insights:** Regularly analyze the performance data from your direct mail campaigns and draw actionable insights. Look for patterns, trends, and opportunities to optimize targeting, messaging, or timing based on the data-driven evidence.

Remember, my dear friend, measuring and optimizing your direct mail campaign is the key to unlocking its full potential. By tracking KPIs, learning from your campaign, and continuously improving, you can achieve greater results and drive the success of your business.

So, let's dive into the world of data, insights, and optimization. Measure, learn, adapt, and watch your direct mail campaigns flourish like never before. May your path to direct mail success be paved with knowledge and growth!

## CHAPTER EIGHT

## The Future of Direct Mail

Welcome to the exciting world of the future, my visionary entrepreneur! In Chapter 8, we explore the ever-evolving landscape of direct mail and how it adapts and thrives in a digital world. Get ready to discover the possibilities, innovations, and the road ahead for this timeless marketing strategy.

**Direct Mail in a Digital World**

In a digital age dominated by online marketing channels, direct mail continues to hold its ground and make a lasting impact. Here's why:

- **Tangible Experience:** Direct mail offers a tangible and tactile experience that digital channels cannot replicate. The physical presence of a well-designed mail piece creates a sense of importance, enhancing the recipient's connection and engagement with your brand.

- **Less Cluttered Environment:** As email inboxes overflow with promotional messages and social media feeds become overcrowded, direct mail provides a refreshing escape. By reaching your audience in a less cluttered environment, you have a higher chance of capturing their attention and standing out from the competition.

- **Personalization and Targeting:** Leveraging customer data and advanced segmentation techniques, direct mail allows for highly personalized and targeted campaigns. By tailoring your message and offers to specific customer segments, you can deliver a more relevant and impactful experience.

## Innovations in Direct Mail

Direct mail continues to evolve and embrace innovations that enhance its effectiveness and efficiency.

Here are some exciting advancements to keep an eye on:

### Variable Data Printing:

Harnessing the power of data, variable data printing enables you to personalize each mail piece with individualized content, images, or offers. This customization creates a sense of exclusivity and relevance, increasing engagement and response rates.

**Augmented Reality (AR):**

By integrating AR technology into your direct mail, you can provide an interactive and immersive experience for your recipients. From 3D product demonstrations to virtual tours, AR adds an exciting element that captivates and engages your audience.

**Integration with Digital Channels:**

Direct mail doesn't exist in isolation. It can be seamlessly integrated with digital channels, such as personalized URLs (PURLs), QR codes, or social media links. These digital integrations enhance the overall customer journey and bridge the gap between offline and online experiences.

**The Road Ahead**

As we gaze into the horizon, the road ahead for direct mail is filled with endless possibilities. Here are some key considerations and trends to embrace:

**Sustainability and Eco-Friendliness:**

With growing environmental consciousness, integrating sustainable practices into your direct mail campaigns is crucial. From using recycled materials to adopting eco-friendly production processes, embracing sustainability aligns with the values of your audience and helps build a positive brand image.

**Enhanced Data Analytics:**

Advancements in data analytics and artificial intelligence open up new avenues for analyzing and leveraging the data generated by direct mail campaigns. By harnessing these technologies, you can gain deeper insights into customer behavior, preferences, and optimize your targeting and messaging strategies accordingly.

## Integration of Personalization and Automation:

The future of direct mail lies in the seamless integration of personalization and automation. By leveraging customer data and automation tools, you can create highly tailored and personalized direct mail campaigns at scale, driving greater efficiency and results.

Embrace the future, my forward-thinking entrepreneur, and unlock the full potential of direct mail in a digital world. By staying informed about innovations, trends, and adopting a customer-centric approach, you can pave the way for direct mail to continue its legacy as a powerful marketing tool.

So, fasten your seatbelt and embark on this journey of innovation and exploration. The future of direct mail is bright, and it's yours to shape. May you navigate the road ahead with confidence, creativity, and a steadfast commitment to success!

# CHAPTER NINE
## Conclusion: Your Journey to Direct Mail Success

Congratulations, my fellow entrepreneur, on reaching the final chapter of this incredible journey towards direct mail success. Throughout this book, we have explored the ins and outs of direct mail, uncovering its power, strategies, and techniques that can elevate your marketing efforts to new heights.

Now, as we conclude this adventure, let

us reflect on the key takeaways and set our sights on the path ahead.

## Direct Mail: A Timeless Marketing Strategy

Direct mail has stood the test of time, and for good reason. It offers a unique and personalized approach that cuts through the digital noise and creates a lasting impression. By leveraging the tactile experience, precise targeting, and creative storytelling, you have the ability to captivate your audience and drive meaningful connections.

## Crafting Your Direct Mail Strategy

Crafting a successful direct mail campaign requires careful planning, understanding your audience, building compelling messages, and presenting them with flair. By following the step-by-step guide provided in this book, you now have the tools and knowledge to create impactful direct mail campaigns that yield exceptional results.

## Measuring and Optimizing Your Campaign

The success of your direct mail campaigns lies not only in their execution but also in the ability to measure, analyze, and optimize their performance. By defining key performance indicators (KPIs), learning from your campaign data, and continuously improving your strategies, you can ensure long-term success and maximize your return on investment.

## Embracing the Future of Direct Mail

As we step into the future, direct mail continues to evolve, adapt, and integrate with digital technologies. Innovations such as variable data printing, augmented reality, and enhanced data analytics open up exciting possibilities for creating more personalized and engaging experiences. By embracing these advancements and staying ahead of industry trends, you can position yourself at the forefront of direct mail excellence.

In conclusion, dear entrepreneur, direct mail is a powerful tool in your marketing arsenal. It allows you to connect with your audience on a deeper level, cut through the digital clutter, and deliver a memorable brand experience. By following the principles and strategies outlined in this book, you are equipped with the knowledge and skills to embark on a successful journey in the world of direct mail.

So, go forth with confidence, creativity, and an unwavering commitment to excellence. Embrace the power of direct mail, nurture your customer relationships, and watch your business flourish. Remember, your journey to direct mail success is ongoing. Stay curious, stay innovative, and keep exploring new ways to captivate and engage your audience.

May your direct mail campaigns be the catalyst for growth, success, and a future filled with endless possibilities. Wishing you all the best on your remarkable journey to direct mail success!

# APPENDIX

## Resources and Further Reading

Congratulations on completing your journey through the world of direct mail! As you continue to expand your knowledge and refine your direct mail strategies, it's important to have access to valuable resources and further reading materials.

In this appendix, we provide a curated list of resources that will serve as your go-to reference for all things direct mail. Whether you're seeking practical tips, in-depth case studies, or industry insights, these resources will help you stay informed and inspired.

### Books
- "The Direct Mail Solution" by Craig Simpson and Dan S. Kennedy
- "Direct Mail in the Digital Age" by Brian Kurtz
- "Successful Direct Marketing Methods" by Bob Stone and Ron Jacobs
- "Direct Mail Copy That Sells!" by Herschell Gordon Lewis

### Online Guides and Articles
- Direct Marketing Association (DMA): Visit the DMA website for comprehensive guides, case studies, and industry reports on direct mail.
- USPS Business Mail 101: Explore the USPS website for detailed information on business mail requirements, rates, and best practices.
- MarketingProfs: This online resource offers a wealth of

articles, webinars, and guides on various marketing topics, including direct mail.

## Industry Associations and Events

- American Marketing Association (AMA): Join the AMA to connect with other marketers and gain access to their resources, events, and publications.
- Direct Marketing Association (DMA): Stay connected with the DMA to stay up-to-date with the latest trends, research, and networking opportunities in direct marketing.

## Direct Mail Service Providers

- USPS Every Door Direct Mail (EDDM): Utilize the USPS EDDM service to reach specific neighborhoods or ZIP codes with your direct mail campaigns.
- Printing and Mailing Companies: Research local or online printing and mailing companies that offer direct mail services. They can help

with design, printing, and mailing logistics.

**Online Communities and Forums**
- Direct Mail Success Forum: Engage with fellow marketers, share experiences, and gain insights from industry professionals in this online community.
- LinkedIn Groups: Join relevant LinkedIn groups focused on direct mail marketing to connect with peers and participate in discussions.

Remember, the learning journey never ends, and there is always more to discover and explore in the realm of direct mail. Continuously seek out new resources, stay updated with industry trends, and adapt your strategies accordingly. Direct mail is a dynamic and ever-evolving field, and staying informed will ensure that you remain at the forefront of innovation and success.

*Happy reading, learning, and implementing!*

# Thank you!

*Thank you so much for being a part of my literary journey and allowing me to share my thoughts and insights with you.*

*I strive to create books that provide value and contribute to the knowledge and understanding of various topics. Your feedback is incredibly valuable to me and plays a vital role in shaping my writing style and the subjects I explore.*

*At OSTRICH, we greatly appreciate the feedback we receive from readers like you. It helps us improve and deliver content that is engaging and meaningful.*

*We are committed to our mission of*

*creating captivating and informative material, and your input is instrumental in achieving that goal.*

*I invite you to visit our website at www.ostrichpress.com or check out our books on platforms like Amazon, Kobo, and Google Play. Your thoughts and opinions matter to us, and we would love to hear your feedback on this book or any others you may have read.*

*Once again, thank you for your support and for being a part of this journey. Your engagement and feedback are truly appreciated.*

*Warm regards,*
*Frank Dappah*

## ABOUT THE AUTHOR

*Frank is a charismatic and visionary entrepreneur, accomplished author, and seasoned investor. With a passion for business and a wealth of experience, Frank has written extensively on topics ranging from marketing and social media to entrepreneurship and beyond. His insightful books have garnered praise for their practical advice and actionable strategies.*

*Living in the vibrant city of Charlotte, North Carolina, Frank thrives on the dynamic energy of the business world. Alongside his partner and wife, Bernice, he has built successful ventures and continues to explore new opportunities in the ever-evolving landscape of entrepreneurship.*

*Frank's unique perspective and expertise make him a sought-after speaker and advisor, empowering aspiring entrepreneurs to unlock their full potential. With his engaging writing style and knack for simplifying complex concepts, Frank has helped countless readers navigate the challenges and seize the opportunities that come with starting and growing their own businesses.*

*When he's not immersed in his entrepreneurial endeavors, Frank enjoys spending quality time with his family, exploring the outdoors, and indulging his love for movies, books, and astronomy. His curiosity knows no bounds, and he is always eager to delve into new subjects and expand his knowledge.*

*Connect with Frank on social media and*

*join him on this exciting journey of innovation, growth, and success.*

*Linkedin: https://bit.ly/3q3llyt*

**OSTRICH**

# RECOMMENDED READING

**Customer Journeys: Why every Startup needs a Customer Advisory Board.**

*What happens when you listen to your customers? What happens when you build a customer-centric startup? - One that is intricately connected to its customers and all the men and women whose lives are impacted every day by your products and services?*

**STATUS UPDATE**

*Strategic social media marketing can be the cure-all your business needs to reach the right audience at the right time. STATUS UPDATE is an easy-to-digest guide to help any Life and/or Health agent or agency make the most of their Facebook marketing system.*

'STATUS UPDATE' is a must-read for any Insurance Agency owner or Broker looking for unique ideas on how to get the most out of their Facebook marketing - Guillossi Asempa

**How to generate and convert health and life insurance sales leads with Facebook Ads**

**FRANK DAPPAH**

Small business social media marketing guide

**CONTINUOUS CONNECTIVITY: Leveraging the power of text messaging to grow your business and enhance your brand reach.**

*I have always considered Sales and Marketing to be that which is most vital to the Startup success and growth of any organization - both at the for profit and nonprofit level. You can have the best ice cream, or coffee in town.*

*Find these and many other titles from the author at Amazon.com, Ostrichpress.com, or wherever you buy books.*

**OSTRICH**®

# Ostrich Publishers

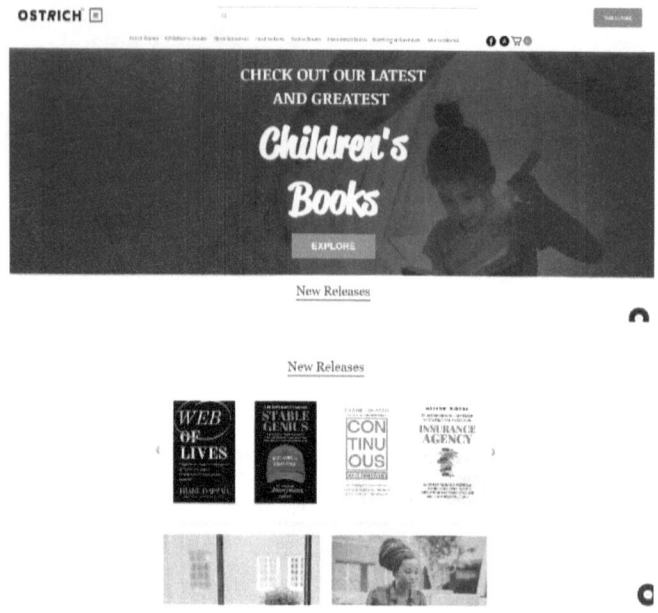

*OSTRICH Publishers (https://www.ostrichpress.com/)*

We have a burning passion for books that runs through our veins and fuels our every endeavor. Books are our sustenance, our oxygen, and our driving force. At OSTRICH, we are dedicated to building a comprehensive publishing and distribution platform that embraces the diversity of authors and creatives from all walks of life.

**Our mission is clear:** to establish OSTRICH as a powerful digital publisher that provides a vibrant platform for talented independent authors and creatives to share their remarkable works with the world. We believe that every voice deserves to be heard, and we strive to create an inclusive space where authors can thrive and connect with their readership on a global scale.

At OSTRICH, we offer a range of services to support authors throughout their publishing journey. We collaborate closely with authors from diverse backgrounds, guiding them through the entire process of bringing their creations to life. From the initial brainstorming phase to the meticulous crafting of their manuscripts, and from distribution logistics to strategic marketing campaigns, we are there every step of the way.

Our dedication extends beyond mere publication. We are committed to empowering authors, who may otherwise go unnoticed, by providing them with the necessary tools, resources, and exposure to reach a wider audience. With our robust distribution infrastructure, we ensure that their finished products reach readers across the globe, transcending geographical boundaries and cultural barriers.

At OSTRICH, we are building more than just a publishing and distribution platform; we are creating a community of passionate authors and readers who share a love for literature and a hunger for knowledge. Join us on this incredible journey as we revolutionize the world of publishing and champion the voices that deserve to be heard. Together, let us soar to new heights of literary excellence.

**OSTRICH PUBLISHERS**

Published by Ostrich Publishing Group

Charlotte, North Carolina 28212, U.S.A

First published in the United States of America by Ostrich Publishing Group, an Independent Book publisher.

9798395556516

Copyright © 2022 Ostrich Publishers

www.ostrichpress.com

All rights reserved.

ISBN: 9798395556516

Except in the United States of America, this book is sold subject to the conditions that is shall not, by way of trade or otherwise, be lent, re-sold, hired out, or otherwise circulated without the publisher's prior consent in any form of binding or cover other than in which is it published and without a similar condition including this condition being imposed on the subsequent purchaser.

# THE MAGIC OF DIRECT MAIL

**OSTRICH**

www.ingramcontent.com/pod-product-compliance
Lightning Source LLC
Chambersburg PA
CBHW020437220526
45464CB00002B/739